MYTHICAL CREATURES

Unicorns

Abby Colich

Raintree

Chicago, Illinois

www.heinemannraintree.com
Visit our website to find out
more information about
Heinemann-Raintree books.

To order:
☎ Phone 888-454-2279
▭ Visit www.heinemannraintree.com
to browse our catalog and order online.

Edited by Adrian Vigliano, Rebecca Rissman,
  and Nancy Dickmann
Designed by Joanna Hinton Malivoire
Levelling by Jeanne Clidas
Original illustrations by Christian Slade
Picture research by Elizabeth Alexander
Production by Victoria Fitzgerald
Printed and bound in China by CTPS

14 13 12 11 10
10 9 8 7 6 5 4 3 2 1

**Library of Congress Cataloging-in-
Publication Data**
Colich, Abby.
  Unicorns / Abby Colich.
    p. cm.—(Mythical creatures)
  Includes bibliographical references and index.
  ISBN 978-1-4109-3800-8 (hc)—ISBN 978-1-4109-
3807-7 (pb) 1. Unicorns—Juvenile literature. I.
Title.
  GR830.U6C65 2011
  398.24'54—dc22   2009052411

Acknowledgments
The author and publishers are grateful to the
following for permission to reproduce copyright
material: Alamy pp. **17** (© Hemis), **18**
(© ArkReligion.com); Bridgeman pp. **11** (National
Museum of Karachi, Karachi, Pakistan), **24** (Private
Collection/ © Look and Learn); Corbis pp. **9**
(© Stapleton Collection), **21** (© The Gallery Collection),
22 (© Alinari Archives), **29** (© Buddy Mays); Getty
Images pp. **7** (Hulton Archive), **28** (Paul Nicklen/
National Geographic); Photolibrary pp. **13** (Stapleton
Historical Collection/Imagestate), **23** (E&E Image Library/
Imagestate), **25** (DEA Picture Library); Shutterstock pp. **8**
(© vincent369), **10** (© Linn Currie).

Every effort has been made to contact copyright
holders of any material reproduced in this book.
Any omissions will be rectified in subsequent
printings if notice is given to the publisher.

Disclaimer
All the Internet addresses (URLs) given in this book
were valid at the time of going to press. However, due
to the dynamic nature of the Internet, some addresses
may have changed, or sites may have changed or
ceased to exist since publication. While the author and
publisher regret any inconvenience this may cause
readers, no responsibility for any such changes can be
accepted by either the author or the publisher.

Some words are shown in bold, **like this**. You can find
out what they mean by looking in the glossary.

Contents

What Is a Mythical Creature?

People all over the world tell stories about **mythical** creatures. The word *mythical* comes from the word **myth**. A myth is a story that is not true.

This is a dragon. It is a mythical creature.

What other mythical creatures can you think of?

werewolf

What Is a Unicorn?

What comes to mind when you think of a unicorn? You may have seen unicorns that look like a white horse with one horn.

Unicorns can have the body of many different animals. But they always have one horn.

The Unicorn's Special Powers

Many **legends** say that the unicorn's horn has special powers. Others say that the unicorn brings people peace, strength, and bravery.

Chinese unicorn statues

DID YOU KNOW?

In some **myths**, unicorns are very hard to catch!

The Unicorn Myth

Myths about the unicorn began thousands of years ago. Stories about the unicorn probably come from horned animals such as:

- antelopes
- deer
- goats
- oxen
- rhinoceroses

rhinoceros

This is a very old clay artwork of a unicorn. It was made between the years 2500 and 1700 BCE.

Ancient Greek Writers

The first people to tell stories of unicorns were the Greeks. One story says that unicorns have the body of a donkey. It also says that unicorns have dark red heads with blue eyes. Their horns are white, red, and black.

Ancient Greece

DID YOU KNOW?

The Greeks named a group of stars monoceros (say *mon-oh-sare-us*). *Monoceros* is the Greek word for unicorn.

Unicorns of the Middle East

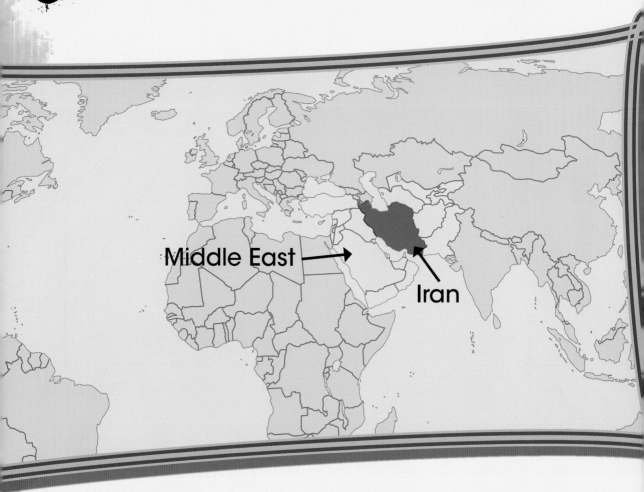

Middle East →

Iran

Legends from the Middle East tell us about a unicorn called the karkadaan (say *car-kuh-dan*). It was a fierce creature that could kill an elephant. The word *karkadaan* means "lord of the desert."

DID YOU KNOW?

People from Persia, now called Iran, believed in a unicorn called the Shadhavar (say *shad-huh-var*). Its **hollow** horn makes music and has a face on it.

Unicorns of Asia

One **legend** in India tells of a creature called Risharinga (say *rish-uh-ring-uh*). He was the son of a man and an antelope. Stories say Risharinga married a princess named Shanta (say *shan-tah*). He saved her father's kingdom from **drought**.

Risharinga

Shanta

Asia

China→

Japan

India↗

DID YOU KNOW?
Indian unicorn stories might
have started because of the
Indian rhinoceros.

Legends in Asia tell about a creature called the Qilin (say *kee-lin*). There are many stories about what the Qilin looks like. But most say it has scales and a horn.

This is a Qilin from China.

kirin

DID YOU KNOW?
The Qilin has many different names. In Japan it is called the kirin (say *kee-rin*).

Unicorns of Europe

There are many **legends** about unicorns in **medieval** Europe. These unicorns usually looked like a goat or a horse with a horn. Some people believed that powder made from a unicorn horn could protect from poison and cure diseases.

Germany

Europe

This well-known cloth from medieval Europe shows a woman and a unicorn.

Myths tell us that unicorns are hard to catch! In some stories, a unicorn can be caught if it lays its head on a **maiden's** lap. Some stories say that unicorns come back to life after being killed.

Unicorns and lions are used in family symbols. Unicorns make people feel strong and brave.

DID YOU KNOW?
Einhorn is the German word for unicorn.

Close Relatives

A **mythical** creature that is like the unicorn is Pegasus. Like some unicorns, Pegasus has the body of a horse. But Pegasus has wings and no horn.

DID YOU KNOW?

These ancient **extinct** animals are named after a mythical beast called the indrik (say *in-drick*). Russian **myths** say the indrik lived on a mountain and ruled all animals.

Could Unicorns Exist?

What do you think?

 They could be real...
- People all over the world tell stories about unicorns.

 I'm not so sure...
- These stories were probably made up about real animals that had one horn.

 They could be real...
- Some people claim they have found unicorn horns.

 I'm not so sure...
- These horns were actually **tusks** from an animal called the narwhal.

They could be real...

- **Legends** say that unicorns are difficult to capture. They might just be really good at hiding from humans.

 I'm not so sure...

- No one has ever actually seen a unicorn.

The truth is unicorns aren't real. But there are many interesting stories about them!

Reality Versus Myth

Narwhal (real)

Found: Arctic Ocean

Lives: In water

Seen: Rarely by humans

Special power: Finds its way using **echolocation**

Narwhals are sometimes called "unicorns of the sea." They are whales with a long, spiraled **tusk**.

Unicorn (myth)

Found: In stories from Asia, Europe, and the Middle East

Lives: On land

Seen: Never by humans

Special power: Protects people from poison and disease

Glossary

drought when a place has almost no rain or water

echolocation using the sound of echoes to find the way

extinct has completely died out

hollow not filled with anything

legend traditional story that may or may not be true

maiden an unmarried woman

medieval period of time in Europe from around the year 500 to around the year 1500

myth traditional story, often about magical creatures and events

mythical found in myths

tusk a long tooth that grows from the jaw in some animals. Some tusks look like horns.

Find Out More

Books

Baynes, Pauline. *Questionable Creatures: A Bestiary*. Grand Rapids, MI: Eerdmans, 2006.

Hamilton, John. *Unicorns and Other Magical Creatures*. Edina, MN: ABDO, 2005.

Knudsen, Shannon. *Fantastical Creatures and Magical Beasts*. Minneapolis, MN: Lerner, 2010.

Websites

www.amnh.org/exhibitions/mythiccreatures/
The American Museum of Natural History's Mythic Creature exhibit Website has lots of information about creatures of the land, sky, and water.

www.fieldmuseum.org/mythiccreatures/index.html
Learn about Dragons, Unicorns, and Mermaids at the Field Museum's Mythic Creatures Exhibit Website.

www.metmuseum.org/explore/Unicorn/unicorn_inside.htm
The Metropolitan Museum of Art's Website has lots of pictures and information about unicorn art called tapestries.

Index